GRACE RUTO is twenty-nine years old. Following the passing away of her father, which was a tragedy for her close-knit family, there commenced the brink and birth of her sensitive nature, which emanated from conspicuous acquaintances and other friendships.

In her studies, she pursued fashion design and received certificates for her academic excellence and an award for being fashion representative of the Student Government Association at the American Intercontinental University. It was while she was at this university that she began to branch out into expression in both her studies and in writing.

This collection of poems is the cultivation of a long-awaited dream come true – to be a poet.

ENCHANTING ECHOES

ENCHANTING ECHOES

Grace Ruto

ATHENA PRESS
LONDON

ENCHANTING ECHOES
Copyright © Grace Ruto 2006

Border design by The Medieval Scribe © 1993
www.medievalscribe.com

All Rights Reserved

No part of this book may be reproduced in any form
by photocopying or by any electronic or mechanical means,
including information storage or retrieval systems,
without permission in writing from both the copyright
owner and the publisher of this book.

ISBN 1 84401 832 6

First Published 2006 by
ATHENA PRESS
Queen's House, 2 Holly Road
Twickenham TW1 4EG
United Kingdom

Printed for Athena Press

*I dedicate my first poem to Ken Roberts for helping me realise my true potential, and most of all, for believing in me –
I love you, Ken!*

Acknowledgment

> Families are wonderful.
> They embrace the bad,
> And celebrate the good,
> And would do all they can, if they could,
> For each other, for always,
> For ever fruitful!

For Mum, Rose Ruto, my brothers, Tony and Ricky Ruto, and my sister, Vicky Ruto.

And for Dad, Joseph K A Ruto, who passed on. I know our love will last for ever and that he will always be in my heart.

Contents

Introduction	xiii
Dispersed Sands	15
Dilemma of a Wish	19
The Mask of God	20
The Undying Bond	21
Time Will Unite Us	22
Secure in the Star	23
Exhumation of Loneliness	24
Memories that Remain	26
Unquestionable Decadence	27
The Visible Enigma	28
Farewell, Christian!	29
My Fantastic Idol	30
Yearning	31
Heartening Recovery	32
Sacrificial Fortitude	33
Time-honoured Endorsement	34
Jeopardised Convolution	35
Sovereign Safety	36
Estimated Endurance	37
Complete Conciliation	38

The Cleansing Castigation	39
The Kind Euphony	40
Severely Heartbreaking Diligence	41
Pre-eminent Peril	43
Displeasing, Distressful Perpetuation	44
Life's Demise	45
Gale of Torture	47
Onerous Knockout	48
Solemn Diffidence	49
Song of the Dead	50
Explicit Expiration	51
Statutory Scope of a Saga	52
The Perturbed Veil	53
Pacifying Parallel	54
The Morning Glory Awakes	55
Unequivocal Condition	56
Sensational Speculation	57
Sermon of Acclimatisation	58
Blunt Debilitation	59
My First Song	60
Tenacious Taciturnity	61
Labour of Love	62
My Saddest Dream	64
Vital Impression	66
Wishful Whispers	67

Selfless Salvage	68
Eagles' Eyes	70
The External Embrace	71
Phenomenal Promise	73
Hope Asunder	74
Fortunate Affection	75
My Darling	76
Empty Words, Empty Promises	77
Eternal Embrace	78
My Life…	80
The Bridge	81
There's No Price I Won't Pay	82
So Sad	83
Two Extremes	84
From Now Until For Ever	85
One…	86
Where Were You?	87
Blue	88
Vindication	89
Solitude	90
Solace…	91
Adversity	92
Release	93
Tragedy	94
Memories	95

Now	96
You…	97
Me…	98
True	99
Since	100
How?	101
Oblivion	102
Days	103
Thoughts	104
Conflict	105
Moments	108
Happiness	109
May 4th	110

Introduction

POETRY

A distinct parenthesis resides in poetry. The boundaries of the future and past are set free and they are made whole by concise description and complete persuasion. It is not that the parade welcomes new feelings which are despatched through poetry, but that the sensitive nature of the soul is acknowledged and pursued.

The difference between truth and lies is manifested by any gifted poet. I sincerely hope that the day will come when the sun escapes the horizon and become my life. Days are traces of the master plan we all adhere to, and therefore must coincide with belief. Categorising the experiences will match up to my life story, and in effect, will make me complete.

So it is for me that I create this book. It is inevitable that time will finish what it began, and light will subdue the earth, mind, heart and spirit. The spirit is part of the soul and they are inseparable – this is my staunch conviction about life. From the beginning, God said, 'Let there be...' – and there was. So this implies to me that you should protect what there is: what you hold true.

Desires are reflected in and manipulated by the mind. The body repels negativity naturally – like bad food – so beware of pretences and affection easily bestowed; it means that your pleasure is the reverse of pain.

We are just beginning a new century with ancient methodologies. Even anachronisms foretell what you must do. This is what I must do – make you all believe. Crossroads of believing in love after all that love has put my heart through. I need to hope again that love will find me. Hope exists and so despair will disappear.

It is to all those people who have inspired me in any way that I owe gratitude. I dedicate this book to all of you. I wish to thank you for expanding my adventures from within.

My mind will now soar like an eagle and hit the bull's-eye of despair. But I shall then be special to you as you all are to me.

Dispersed Sands

In the fair green of summertime
I run to shore where the waters were wet,
Between the dawn and the daytime.
The summer was glad that we met.

There was something the season wanted –
Though the air smelt sweet,
The breath of our lips that parted,
The pulse of the grass at your feet,

You came, and the sun came after,
And the mild dew golden above,
And the daisies lightened with laughter,
And the meadow sweet shook with love.

What shall be said between us here
Among the downs, between the trees,
In fields that knew our feet last year?
In sight of quiet sands and seas?

As a fire of flowers and glowing grass,
In the old fields we could laugh and linger,
Seeing each our souls
In last year's glass.

Shall we not laugh,
Shall we not weep?
Not we,
Though this be as it is?

For love awake or love asleep,
Ends in a laugh, a dream, a kiss –
A song like this –

I that slept awake in love,
In a dream though love do all that love can do,
My heart will never ache nor break
For your heart's sake.

The great sea,
Faultless as a flower,
Throbs, trembling under beam and breeze,
And laughs with love of the amorous hour.

I've found love's new name good enough,
But less sweet than you –
I've found the sweetest name that ever
Love grew weary of –

Birds quick to fledge,
My heart quick to pledge,
And quick to call,
And to fall…to fall for you –

And in my soul lies a hunger for love.
No diver brings up love again,
Once dropped in such cold seas
That's gone deeper than all plummets sound.
Where in the dim green dayless day,
I question and plead
For love that was true.

Like colours in the sea, like flowers,
I wait for love for hours,
And soft like sighs –
And all these,
Like your name, Ken.

O lips of mine that daydream about
Kissing you;
O fervent eyelids letting through
Those eyes, the bluest of all skies.

If you were I,
And I were you,
Would the day love nightfall and her dew,
Though night may love the day?

Love is hard to seize.
So take the season and let love
Fill the hours,
And our two souls may sleep
And wake up one;
Or dream, they wake
And find it so.
Then we'll know –
And I would say,
Kiss me once,
Hard as though a flame,
Lay on my lips and make them fire,
The same lips, now
Not the same.
What breath shall fill and re-inspire
My desire,
But you?

Immortal are they,
Clothed with powers,
Gods over all the fruitless hours,
Too great to appease,
Too high to appal,
Too far to call.

Yet we have called upon them
Since the sands fell through time's
Hourglass first –
A seed of life.
And out of many lands,
Have we stretched hands.

Doth heaven murmur
And repeat
Sad sounds or sweet?
Do the stars answer
In the night when I'm all alone
And craving an embrace?
What hope, what light,
When searching for an eternal companion?

True love
Is like a barren blossom
Filled with ghosts of words
And dusty dreams,
Though love will avail,
As we watch the same fields and skies!

Dilemma of a Wish

Could it be?
Two hearts, two minds, one wish –
Feeling this desire for you growing in me –
This burning sensation can't be fulfilled by a dish.

With every breath I take,
I'm swallowed up by thoughts of you next to me.
It seems like your presence would be enough to make
My lonely, hollow eyes see.

How two thoughts can unite,
And how spirits can join,
Deep and dark in the night.
I'll take this pen and on my soul I shall sign.

My life to be with you.
Now that we have happy memories,
Tell me if you feel it too,
'Cause what I know now is empty reveries.

I'll close my eyes
And picture you in my dream,
But it's so hard to hold the pillow when my heart cries.
I just can't make-believe, and if I could, it would seem

Pointless and cruel to my fragile heart,
Unfair and emotionally draining to my mind.
So this one wish could be mine, or yours, or fate –
'Cause I don't know when I shall see you again,
But I'm hoping that your love
Shall one day in my heart find.

The Mask of God

You have to believe to receive
Is what I heard,
But time hasn't been kind to me;
The pain of believing left me for dead.

Tears just stream down my face
When I think of believing in my dream.
The pain comes alive each time I embrace
That one dream that's swept me away in its stream.

I refuse to give up hope,
And this is why it hurts so bad.
If only my knight in shining armour could come and elope
With me in his arms, with a blessing from God.

All my dreams have come true in my head,
But reality faults me each time.
Heartache and dread,
I can now hear the whispering cold wind chime.

I'd rather walk on fire
Than go through this.
But this option would kill my desire,
And together with it the pain would ease.

I'll just watch my heart leap for joy,
When I know I shall live to see my dream fulfilled.
I'll save my fears for later and cry,
And wait for the day when my pain shall be healed.

The Undying Bond

It's been a while
Since I let you into my heart.
It's about time we walked down that aisle.
I could blame it all on young cupid's dart,
But it felt so right
From the start till now.
You'll always be my guiding light.
Whatever I reap, I know I shall sow.
When I weep
Those God-forsaken tears,
Your strength in me I shall keep,
Each time to silence my fears.
You share every joy
And every sorrow.
Each and every whisper of your advice I shall employ;
You are my tomorrow.
My past lay hidden in your power,
My present time is completed by you,
My future belongs with you, every minute, every hour.
Your love for me shows in everything you do.
The way that we are,
I know we'll last for all eternity.
It's marked in our star
And sealed in reality.
No matter whether we are apart,
Our hearts beat as one.
Time has confirmed to my soul that we'll never depart
From this heaven I've found in my dream man.
I pledge my life, spirit and soul,
To be yours truly.
Before God and His angels in all
That I am His fully.

Time Will Unite Us

I realise it is too late.
Your love shines right through my eyes
So I'll just have to embrace my fate,
And even the trial that tries
To separate the new fresh life I radiate
That began when you took my place,
And unlocked my heart to emancipate
The once naïve stagnation of my face.
And you instilled in me joy
That I never imagined I'd experience.
You are my sole salvation, my envoy.
My soul your entrance,
Day after day.
You show me that you'll never leave me.
No hesitation, no delay,
You always came through for me, and now you'll be
The director of my destiny,
With God as the overhead.
I never could view you with scrutiny,
And if in the end I'm blinded, it may be said –
'Cause my love for you will never change –
It's a price I'll innocently pay
Just like the cost of loving you caused my mind to
  derange.
All I can hear my breath say is,
'I love you…'
Each whisper is a token of our commitment,
And you'll always be true,
So every breath I take shall prove to you all that is meant
To reconcile my fate with your hope,
Our hope that we'll always be together.
Right now, alone without you, I'll try to cope
Until the moment we are united when the angels gather.

Secure in the Star

The love sealed in me,
And that one star that was you,
And even if you can never be,
Our hearts will for ever be true.
We'll make our home in the sea;
Both of us too,
Shall hide and flee
And try to woo
The Power Almighty so that He
Can pardon our sin that we don't rue,
Because finding each other brought the greatest glee,
And so my soul flew
To unite with you, and at once I was free.
At that instant I knew
That my soul shall see
The home for us two,
Far, far away from the tree
That hid the conventional lore askew.
Which reality mocked my dreams to disagree,
And turned life's view
Into a frightening future that's dreary.
And you, my love, were all I could pursue.
Time has made my heart weary,
Yet you gave me a dazzling milieu,
And with you my life was cheery.
And in that final hour when the clocks review,
Details of my past will nullify.
They will plead my case in lieu
So that God's law will not vilify,
But welcome our unification with his crew,
And not condemn us but tally,
Because destiny chose us and so we drew.

Exhumation of Loneliness

I lay down my life as a gift.
You came into my life, and for my sake,
You gave me something solid I can hold that would lift
My spirits to console, and through and through make
My broken life mend
And my crippled words at ease.
Your love in my heart would lend
Your wisdom and enthusiasm in a kiss
That wiped away all sorrow,
Hidden in my mind.
Each time I surrendered to tomorrow,
You were the only one who was kind
And understanding of my tears.
You would restore and guide
My deserted existence through the years.
You gave me the love I always dreamt about,
Even though I never thought I'd deserve you,
I shall stay devout.
To you I will yield so true
And completely,
Until time ends.
Just as you swore to me lately
That, even though reality tends
To discourage and disillusion me,
Our love shall stand the test of time,
And the whole earth shall see
How you and I were as inseparable as a rhyme,
And your life is mine to guard,

With my life, which is for you to shield.
Charging forth with the vanguard,
Battling with disbelief and doubt in the field,
I shall offer my life as a connection with you,
Never knowing but still believing that a man doesn't go into
A battle to win, because defeat is an eclipse.

Memories that Remain

Happy times seem clouded,
Angels all are gathered
To hold on to the past,
To be blinded as the future can last,
To betrothe the tears of sadness,
To release the frustrations of gladness,
As today there's so much,
So say it and in your heart search
For the special moments
That turned your life around – for no laments
For good ones inspire hope,
Bad ones reminisce, leaving a gap
Of what stands in the way,
Of sorrow to quench and then light in a ray
Of candles to relinquish
Sad times left to banish,
Love to avail,
Hearts to revel,
Belief to re-inspire,
Hope left as a desire,
And happiness as a lure!

Unquestionable Decadence

My heart longs to forgive you the suffering you caused.
I never thought a sorrow so deep could befall,
But my mind could never forgive – you are still accused.
Trying – feels like I'm slamming my head on the wall!
The pain cuts through my being,
And ruptures in my brain.
Frustration and anger are often deceiving.
My instinct is to refrain,
Escape from those haunting thoughts
Of self-pity and self-loathing.
Your wilful self-proclaimed glory rots;
This inconsiderate treatment leaves my mind meditating.
Your presence is a constant reminder
Of the love between us you've betrayed
For the world to see you as a virtuous reviver.
When all that happened was a dispute that strayed,
And as insignificant as the downcast.
You robbed my future before my very eyes,
The endearment between us is in the past.
This tiny eye spies
The colossal pride you believe in.
You command me to sacrifice my freedom to abide,
Yet I was closer to you than to kin.
Today, because of you, I go through my life vapid.
Not even God could have changed your mind –
I shall now call you the director of my doom.
I wish this episode never happened so I could find
A place in my heart, just a little room.
The lights of my world are now flickering,
My soul is now offering
Its existence for the extraordinary that promises
   nurturing.
My calm solitude is evidence of my caring.

The Visible Enigma

Many people confuse money with integrity;
The integrity of any man is not a measure
Of his treasure –
It would instead be called vanity.
Many people confuse fate with destiny;
The destiny of man is to revere himself,
His true self,
And not give in to self-delusion.
Many people confuse instinct with love;
Love is the sum of instinct and feeling
That is willing
To surrender to the wings of a dove.
Many people confuse joy with laughter;
Laughter is a spontaneous reaction
From imagination,
Manifesting from the Almighty Creator.
Many people confuse desire with passion;
Passion glows like a fire
That will never tire.
It brings wholeness to the soul or devours it in completion.
Many people confuse pain with anger;
Anger comes from a fear,
A twisted idea
That begins the state of great anxiety and hunger.
Many people confuse sadness with loneliness;
Loneliness exists because of a situation
Lacking intention,
That can lead a sober man into senselessness.
Many people confuse calmness with tranquillity;
Tranquillity is nothing but a well-ordered mind,
A rare find;
It differentiates between inferiority and superiority.

Farwell Christian!

You probably take me for a fool,
Now that we no longer speak.
What you've done is cruel –
Guess I came across to you as a freak.
No excuses, no remorse,
Your lure, my cure, together a divorce.
My wish almost came true,
Believing in you,
But you probably played a game,
Unfair, yet enjoyable.
You ignited a flame.
It's just that believing in our fantasy is regrettable.
My words, you would never criticise,
My life you would recognise;
You reconciled my wish with hope.
I watched my heart flop,
I chose not to resist.
Your proposal was promising,
But now the matter is closed, I shall not persist.
Your memory is now vanishing,
It's good that we are distant.
I was obviously not important,
So I shall wish you well.
I surrender to the toll of the bell,
And for better or worse,
You will be my treasure,
'Cause it was all a farce.
I gave our secret away to strangers to relieve the pressure;
That kind of tension
Only brought feelings of rejection,
For all your pretension
Made us both fade at culmination.

My Fantastic Idol

I can still remember our affectionate telepathy
As if it was just yesterday.
I like that you took me in sympathy,
Faster than light you never would delay.
You would comfort me
In the still of the night.
You made me see
The life I dreamed that became my light.
Your love was always perfect
And will always be.
Happy memories make me reflect,
Breathing new life in me with glee,
And now my heart belongs
Where the mountains touch the sky,
And when I shall hear that gong,
I shall fly,
Blindly advancing.
Your love brought back dynamism
Once lost as I had watched my heart exploding
With you, handsome,
Kind-hearted and worthy.
My existence is now wholesome,
In every way you are pithy.
Every moment spent with you is pleasurable –
I just can't wait to be with you for ever.
In my daddy's eyes you will be commendable,
So when I enter the next world I pray our love will deliver
All that this world's reality denied;
Thanks to you it was not more than I could bear.
Enduring the sorrow, I relied
On you emotionally and mentally 'cause you're the only
    one who'd care.

Yearning

Thinking has left me forlorn
Wishing has made me thrown –
By the succour of love's sweet nectar;
By the breath of your sweet kiss there.
To me it seems to call
My heart free to sail;
To squeeze your hand;
To taste the magic that turned
My mind to reach out
To grasp at the night –
So still, so easily escapes –
The stars, moonlight and the wind replace
The dusk with music ringing,
The birds singing,
To be one, to be whole, finally.
You, only you and me truly
Betrothed in tears,
Fearing
To be in love;
And the sky above
Holds us, holds me, and you
Fill the sky blue!

Heartening Recovery

You are my shadow.
I will love you for being so close,
'Cause for ever our love will glow.
Through all my problems you arose,
Conquering all my insecurities
By being faithful.
I was the first one on your list of priorities.
You make my whole being grateful
To have known you for six years;
And still I'm happy to be submissive.
You're my joyful tears
And the pain that is forcefully permissive.
I couldn't live without you,
You're all that I have.
For the rest of my life all I shall view
Is how you came to save
My innocence from the hurt
Of deliverance.
It was my nature to be curt.
You've changed me through your perseverance,
And now my veins feel alive.
My character has new meaning
My true self shall derive
From our mutual understanding,
And together we shall conceive
Our love child.
We don't need to receive
Approval from this guild,
'Cause our direction
Is our fruition,
And our stimulation
Is our unparalleled aspiration.

Sacrificial Fortitude

So you thought medication would alter
All those times I would falter?
Maybe to you I was going mental,
      But to me I was euphorical.
Loneliness finally made me at peace,
But you thought I was about to decease.
The problems you thought I contained
      Were my sustenance towards my beloved,
Who was in turmoil,
Unseen, but I sensed it in my soul.
He and I were in paradise.
      You had to shatter my heroism
With your paranoid whim
That my pearl of quietness
Was indeed a sign of madness.
And so you handed me over to qualified asses
So I could fit in with the masses?
Don't you see I needed you to believe in me
So I could believe in me?
But no!
You turned into my prime foe
'Cause you betrayed my trust
And smiled as I was no longer robust.
But even that strength I never needed
'Cause I'd already surrendered it, premeditated,
To my sole lover
Whose love took over,
Readily through my consent,
That filled me with so much to repent,
'Cause I should have loved him from the start.
Now he means more to me than life
And for ever will live in my heart.

Time-honoured Endorsement

A brainwave of doubt
Escaped my mind.
I knew I could never live without
Knowing and feeling your exuberance in my mind.
You supported my weakness
And made me whole.
You are my most sincere experience
Of the truth and power of love's call.
Flashes of others
Made me think you never wanted to be with me any more.
A chilling isolation bothers
The once calm assurance of for evermore.
Then you closed my eyes
And held me in your arms
And in the morning when I did rise,
I was possessed by your charms
And knew you'd always love me
And I would always love you.
My love, if I should be so lucky to see
The visible form of your debut,
I'll know if I have a destiny
And that destiny is to defy loneliness.
I will have dignity.
You'll be my hero, the epitome of successfulness.
I promise you that nothing can come between us
'Cause you're my life, my mind, my soul.
I live and breath these verses
As an oath of my all,
And of the times we've had
And of the times yet to come.
And when I'll be clad
In white, I shall finally be home.

Jeopardised Convolution

What the hell
Is running through your mind?
You always want to yell
Trying to find
A sign on the road
That leads to love.
So you swam in the flood
Of tears from a dove
Crying to you
To trust in the word,
But your baffled mind seems to easily misconstrue
The reasons why you drown in blood.
And then there is a whisper
That you are stained and scarred.
You hear the unseen cry from your helper,
To whom you've laid down your guard,
And who has promised
You are the one he needs,
And will fulfil all you ever dreamed.
Faithful are all his deeds.
And suddenly
The journey is set.
You proceed melancholy
Because it is him you have never met.
You curse the sky
And isolate yourself from the world.
You wave goodbye
So willingly to hearts untrue to the wish you hold.
With clenched fists
You challenge the Almighty.
You now mock his feats
With vigilant spirituality.

Sovereign Safety

My love, you are so loving
And so deserving.
My heart you purify,
My troubles you nullify.
You make me so happy.
You are so worthy.
I don't want anyone to take your place
Until I shall see your face.
You turn a frown
Into a breathtaking crown
With the power you furnish
That renders all sorrow to banish.
For your love is my life;
Your love spells freedom from strife;
Fear has nowhere to hide
When you are by my side.
Nothing can take your place.
I no longer chase
After the wind
For something to bind
My dream of love
With the star up above
That came shining
When my life was confusing
And no one understood.
The pain I felt without fortitude,
Faking love all round,
Seemed to condemn me, and I drowned
In misery and regret
That resulted in fret
And ended with my soul's inevitable detour.
My love, I needed you; you came and are my saviour!

Estimated Endurance

I keep telling myself,
I won't be caught up again.
It's my goal to be aloof,
So my faith can regain
Its majestic composure,
Worth contemplating,
For long I've suffered exposure.
My face is manifesting
The constraints I've mastered,
Always wishing for someone like you.
I attempted to appear well shadowed,
Unaware that my chosen few
Would rather set their sights elsewhere,
Leaving me to choke in tears intractable.
I keep warning myself that I should be aware
Now I see this fault is redeemable,
'Cause I won't be caught up again
In a battle I can't win.
This time the battle will have to ordain
This ordeal repeating that seems to determine
The climax of my happiness.
'Cause my vulnerable disposition
Intensely deepens my sadness,
As I meditate on vast suppositions
As to why this happens to me,
My confidence dwindles.
I just want to be free
To choose and love someone who rekindles
This dying flame,
Who can say my name,
And treat me like a dame,
But I don't know yet if he came.

Complete Conciliation

I am longing
For that gentle caress,
That unification of knowing,
The wonderful experience of a love that will never erase.
With the heart glowing
And captured in my face,
No more showing
The infliction of scars
Reality was always causing.
Sadness and rejection left a trace
That made me self-demeaning,
Defying my true self to the false.
And my mind started reasoning,
Patronising my innocence,
Resisting the Almighty Power and challenging
The measure of His status.
I started surely dehumanising
The deficit of my existence,
Between wanting
And reluctance
Gave way to anything
That made me relish my longing for an instance.
And I gave away everything,
Including my self-reverence,
For that reviving feeling.
I fell in love in a trance.
My heart is still explaining
Why I chose to dance
With his companionship, in senselessness.
I know I treat him with sensitiveness.
I'm just hoping the joy he brings will be endless!

The Cleansing Castigation

When God made the earth,
He made it burn and turn.
Love made man earn
The sacred mirth.
God is now making new life on the moon
So the process continues.
Love brings the blues,
Colliding with the afternoon.
God is the word,
Which man wrote,
And teachers of the truth taught.
All obedient spirits rise and nod,
Acknowledging that love lives,
And it breeds,
Sowing the seeds
With the power it gives
Through God as the overhead.
Man will sail
And love will prevail
On that final bed,
Until the mystery
Is revealed to man:
Understanding makes the heart run
For dear life, or makes him weary.
'Cause reality is judging
The things undone, commanding,
The mind still hesitating,
The soul left deciding,
Faith still revenging,
Belief left binding,
The body still marching
Towards the unknown, left succeeding!

The Kind Euphony

On my bedside table
There is a plant,
Red and green without a label.
Each time I hunt,
For the reasons of my pain,
I shed tears
That fall like rain,
Tears of fears
That feed my potted flower
And give it life –
The life in me, draining away each hour.
It represents me in its still life.
I use a cup
I drank water from;
I pass my energy to it when I nap.
It breathes my oxygen when I sleep all alone but warm;
It keeps me company
And brightens my days,
Something which cannot be bought with money.
And he speaks to me and says,
'These tears I will bear,
Your fears I will nourish and extinguish.'
He shows me how to truly care.
Yes, my plant, my flower is ready to relinquish
My insecurities caused by solitude.
Heaven knows I'm madly in love,
So he comforts me and offers me fortitude.
My lovely plant drove
My confusion to an end,
And my perseverance to declare
That my emotions it will defend;
Its life from me is a testimony that it will swear.

Severely Heartbreaking Diligence

For You, Morgan

Looks like I fell for you;
Seems like you are me;
One glance and I knew

It's the end of my reverie.

Looks like I've got your number;
I've tried and tried;
Until I drifted into a slumber,

I wanted you so much.

Loving you is my destiny;
I needed to touch
The edge of sanity,

But if this was your intention,

Then thank you for your cruelty;
For the sake of your pretension
I'm the victim in casualty;
'Cause the family brutalised
My aspirations and worth,

Then it's time you realised
That what you did henceforth
Is nothing –
It's only that I'm shattered.
Guess you did mean something.
It's never faltered,
Only treasured the moment

That you were there.
My lifetime of torment
Sent my soul searching everywhere.
If we meet again,
Fate will be too kind,
'Cause my heart will not refrain
From loving you with all my mind –
If you had only given me your right number!

Pre-eminent Peril

I can now see
The wind blowing on my ashes.
Down on one knee,
With flattering lashes,
The wind has taken
And stirred my sorrow.
I feel forsaken,
Like there is no tomorrow.
The crow glides
In the distance so clear.
My soul sides
With love so dear.
The piercing eye of thunder
Fills my need with regret.
Maybe it's my gender –
Weak and vulnerable, yet in debt
For this life
Of mystery,
Full of strife
With no hope of delivery.
No sleight of hand
To sustain
The impossible land
Of uncertainty
Clouded with expectations.
I've been told I'm dainty.
Then why am I alone in this nation
Without a someone to complete
this pattern of love's plan,
Living and breathing,
To whom I can run
When grief is overwhelming
And living is terrifying?

Displeasing, Distressful Perpetuation

Don't assume things about me –
They've taken my dreams and paid the fee.
Yes, my life in a case
Was theirs to unlock
And devour.
They tortured me in a flock
And stole my power.
So don't remind my head
Of the pain lurking,
Deeply killing, that led
To my moments of feeling
Needed, wanted, believed in.
They threw me out,
And sensationalised within
The prison of doubt.
With no one to turn to,
Hit right between the eyes,
They threw my life in the queue
For redemption that dies.
Fulfilling their sole desires,
Deserting and inflicting guilt,
As thoughts flooded and tires
The reverence for myself I built.
Which took nineteen years
To realise my self-worth,
And adjusting to my newly found tears
Of joy that surpassed truth.
They broke my heart
And sucked away my strength in glee
Until now they vaunt
When all I wanted was to be free!

Life's Demise

It's times like these
That make the heart cease,
Not knowing what to do.
Even the things you knew
Cannot console,
The hurt digging its hole –
Inside, within,
Outside where you have been.
The day may still linger
Like the voice of a singer.
Torn and shattered,
The forbidden reality is littered
With happy memories
And with it, life in a series.
My dear,
Please don't shed one more tear
'Cause my heart is with you
And will be true.
I care
And I'll be there.
Distance cannot stop
The truth of hope,
And I won't let sorrow's path
Be the aftermath
Of this tragedy.
So long as I breath I'll try to remedy
This sadness caused
That God has posed
To what purpose no one knows.
Your kindness to me still glows,
And I wish I could be by your side.
Please don't let this tide

Of anguish
Destroy the kindness you furnish,
'Cause losing yourself,
As I did myself,
Will break my heart in two.
I love you,
And I've realised
The lifetime about which I fantasised
With my father,
Changed like the weather,
And living is a rehearsal of the great plan,
And so God makes us learn
This great lesson,
Each of us in person.

Promise me you will take good care of yourself –
'cause living is the best dream you can play.

Gale of Torture

Now that I haven't got a chance,
The intermediary failed,
And your face in me a trace
Of happiness beyond contempt, yet to build,
I see the sky
And a terror beckons.
I tried to lie
But my heart reckons
Your reality cannot be mine,
And so our love cannot exist.
So I'll be fine,
Knowingly applauding the beast
Who stole me
And cast my hope away.
Her name is V
And her eyes portray
Despise and jealousy
Towards me unfounded.
But the ultimate decision is a fallacy
'Cause I feel broken-hearted
When all I wanted
I saw in you.
I now feel haunted
And don't know what to do.
I can still feel your presence,
The symphony of the triumph,
The phoney peril; I can sense
The breeding thoughts that say you're my half
And together we can make a whole,
United we can touch –
My love, I rise and fall.
Looks like you're gone and now I begin a new search.

Onerous Knockout

Just had a beer
And shed a tear
'Cause you're not near.
My world is not clear,
Without you, dear.
Your words I can still hear,
My feelings I still fear –
Lights out and not one cheer.
I try to turn a deaf ear
'Cause it's you I revere,
But I don't want to interfere.
Your kind demeanour
Engraved in me, will devour
My inborn flair
That shows on my exterior
But crumbles in the veneer.
Your gestures were queer.
Experience shown in your picture,
Here in my head an enticing feature;
The end of solitude your overture;
Just you and me – nothing to procure.
I guess your kind of love can expire,
Our destiny a desire
Yet to inspire,
'Cause the epitome of grandeur
Takes away the pressure
And grants pleasure
Undeserved, and rancour.
I still see you in the mire,
I scream to your lost soul's sphere,
And try so hard to steer
This vessel of fire!

Solemn Diffidence

Been sitting here for hours,
Feeling lost again –
Nothing to gain.
I still pick out strange colours
To kill my buried instinct
That always drives me crazy
When all seems hazy –
Many things unsaid still distinct.
And now I've decided
To direct this God-forbidden existence.
For this life he chose to dispense
Proves that happiness has ended.
So I'll be well-disposed,
Teaming up with my enemies,
And judging with merit
Life's jigsaw that can fit,
That can stop this tide of emotional severities;
And leave me alone in an ocean of bliss
To recapture the true meaning of my being,
Endlessly chasing the invisible hand, still fleeing,
Begging for my release,
Anguished and delirious,
Both at the same time.
All my thoughts not worth a dime,
Yet they all seem so serious,
Just touching the sky,
Facing the moon.
It's the dawn of doom in a tune.
I wish I could just fly
Far, far away,
And see the dawn of a new day,
And then everything would be okay!

Song of the Dead

Fan the stars,
Bleed the scars,
Tell the lies
When love dies.
Light the fire,
Rebuke the liar,
Deny you ever asked,
Brag that you passed.
Start the chase
Of a dying phase.
Reflect on dreams,
Burst the seams,
Raise hell
And yell.
Let it all out,
End the bout,
Relive all happy moments
As your hope ferments.
Leave the phone to ring,
Nothing left to fling.
Throw your life on the line
And say you'll be mine.
Resist the angel,
Drown the jingle.
It's Christmas halos,
No longer Christmas carols.
It's time to dine;
Your long-awaited feast is fine.
And your soul is sour
As if you'd even bother,
So reflect on bygones
'Cause we all turn to dust and bones!

Explicit Expiration

Dreams can be a dangerous thing.
Dreams make the mind boil over
Like a dangerous fling.
They can make you run for cover;
Like little thoughts
That are matched with your heart's consent
Like many little boats
That represent
The nature of your soul,
And the anguish if in vain.
They creep up and dig a hole.
And slowly gain
Your countless insecurities,
Which govern your being
Deep down where you hide your amenities,
For fear of seeing
The shell of doubt
Grinning at you from behind.
With a fainting heart you give out
All that you have to the grind,
Disintegrating the foundations
Of contention once a statue.
One by one you make constructions
Of your world in blue,
Green, red and orange,
Until you feel satisfied,
And then you start to fear change
'Cause that beast in a shell justified
Your need to have a dream
So you turn around and try to kill it.
Heart, soul and mind team
And believe it or not, the candle can no longer be lit!

Statutory Scope of a Saga

Tired of all this aggression,
Just want to feel some passion.
Endless days spent in my own world
Searching for gold
Made me want to run,
Wishing I had a chance to turn
To stop the noises ringing
So I can finally hear the birds singing.
I did some paintings
Of idealistic beginnings
To show my self the way
Out of this jungle in the day.
I crawled under my bed at night
So I couldn't see the light,
And then I'd arise
To see the sunrise,
And smile to myself, dazed,
Feeling as pretty as a cake glazed.
Thoughts of tomorrow
Filled me with sorrow
So I started to lock my room
And this was the commencement of my doom,
Because what happened after
Made me burst into laughter
As my mum and dad beat the door down.
Feeling like a clown,
I had to give an explanation,
But I refused in rejection,
So I was warned
To tell the truth – that lesson I never learned
Came from my master,
Who taught me to run faster!

The Perturbed Veil

I loved you the moment I saw you.
Is it true that you've died in combat?
Through the years you made me anew.
In a panic I awoke and my head said: What?
Weak and pained, I slowly walked to the door –
I was about to touch it when I fell
And my head hit the floor.
Tears streamed down my cheeks and I began to yell,
'I'm dying…I'm dying.'
'Cause without you my life is empty,
Void of any hope for living.
Paralysed on the floor, I reached for sanctity,
Begging them to take my life
So we could still be together,
But they cautioned my heart in strife
And said that my breath will be ours for ever.
So I embraced the wind
And sang to the birds.
As I slowly started to regain consciousness, I leaned,
Reaching to you with unspeakable words,
Just groping in the darkness,
Crying and faint.
And in tasting madness
I turned to Renata the saint
And said a silent prayer
That would fix your memory
Of that first moment, till now, I care.
Even though it's just a reverie,
I'll keep you here
Safe in my heart.
I'll try not to shed one more tear
As my life fades from pert!

Pacifying Parallel

Surrealistic living,
My heart still believing
In this form of surrender
That will eventually render
My tears as a sacrifice
To envelope in its vice;
Merging with the spirits,
And never judging their merits;
'Cause my loneliness burns.
Think its magnanimous bondage turns,
Struggling to become me,
Strangling the life that was meant to be.
Breathing my breath,
Conquering the earth,
Convincing my tears
That it will heal my fears.
And in offering my soul
To its promise to make me whole,
I reject humanity
And with it sanity,
And curl up in my hermitage;
Just me and this self-sabotage;
Living together as a married couple;
Unable to open up to people.
We co-exist
And I never resist
The nights of love
Sealed with the cry of a dove,
Screaming for my release
To the heavens to ease
My pain and sorrow
Of this surrealistic tomorrow.

The Morning Glory Awakes

The summer is here –
Looks like the spring haunts and calls him near.
The days begin to rehearse,
The flowers alive and the ecosystem perverse;
Trees seem to linger to the heart
That once stood high as a statue astute,
To look up to ideals
And down on all bended knees,
To try to show the compassion,
To make that decision.
When history ferments,
From mistakes from parents,
Love, peace, harmony, all at once
Seem somehow solemn in this town.
But when time confounds,
The days profound;
Begin the search.
And start the march
To say that ideals are like a moral statue,
Let not goodness fracture,
As summer whispers: 'Times unforeseen,
Times yet to be – let's keep the hope
For a better tomorrow!

Unequivocal Condition

My home will be a nutshell.
I shall put in paintings of my father,
An ode to him whose bell did toll
Not too far in the past.
The day a fixed memory,
His dying moments a seizure,
So with crippled words I cursed the sky.
Uncontrollable tears made me collapse on the bed,
Listless and torn,
Void of any feeling.
This heartbreak alive and seething was to be borne,
But I didn't know how.
With time, I grew conscious.
Living without dad,
I proceeded to become fallacious
And so my home will be a testimony
To make all the world believe
The epitome of strength he was and still is.
While my heart shall relive,
With each brushstroke, I shall show
That he can live for ever
Just as I had planned.
Even though his existence was terminated by the Giver,
I shall prove that life is a destination
Where time decides,
And love is a composition
That binds life with time
Regardless of lifespan.
And distance is no obstacle,
Because what makes a man
Is the legacy left,
Not the peace of heaven's rest!

Sensational Speculation

Déjà vu is no coincidence,
But if I had a preference
I'd call it the sixth sense,
Because it justifies knowing
And instils belonging,
But rebukes believing.
Each man must live his moment
Of exhilaration that stamps out torment
And does not cause detriment.
All hearts that are free reside
In the hollow of eyes that never decide,
But instead, take the chance and ride.
And so vehemence is revealed
When they see reruns of the life once lived
And start to lie that they once believed.
And the writer of the plot
Releases them to see if they can float,
But as the story always goes – they have been bought.
The dark secret of loyalty
Lies in a buried memory,
And then with nothing to rely,
They blindly fight with life's promise,
As if the writer can again accept their fees.
The writer has locked them up and thrown away the key!
Then misery sets in
And doubt sinks in
But it's a one-way road in,
And so they spread the lie
That déjà vu is a pie
That is hidden in the sky
'Cause it's you they want to go down with –
It's you who will be the myth.
When you die they will crown you with a wreath!

Sermon of Acclimatisation

Everything in its own time;
Anything shall come from this;
Nothing worth having is prime.
So all that it is
Could never be enough.
If you choose to hold on,
Knowing that life is rough,
You just have to wait for the dawn,
And until then
Explore your dreams
And try to remain sane,
'Cause luck's beams
Shine for only the chosen.
Better still we're all counted.
Each one's fate shall worsen
If the knife is twisted,
'Cause you are conceived
And your mind directs your soul.
Your body in the end is received
Back to the home you nail,
Banging and breaking.
Your dreams will finish you
Sooner in thinking,
But if you let your mind soar in the queue,
Your demise will be reassuring
And your destiny will be welcoming.
Since no one's ever been able to return,
Your ruined life to adjourn,
To reconcile the day with the night,
And wrong from right.
'Cause you can't fight to reinforce the future,
All you have to do is recompense hearts for all and
　　nurture!

Blunt Debilitation

It's the luck of the draw
That completely screws you up;
Left standing at the door,
Your tears swallowed by the teacup.
You know your days are numbered
And the time races.
The same need has stirred and hammered
Agony – and pessimism laces
The fear, lurking unknown.
Because finding your love is a journey;
Once found will for ever be the dawn
In your eyes. And as eternal as money
The form may change,
But the value shall stand.
You know it's a choice from the range,
Class A, B, or C – whichever is close to hand.
So you make a choice
And rekindle your dying hope.
Controlling your every move is your conscience – voice,
Then the flame dies and you stop
All the yearning,
All the crying.
It's time to rise
And take charge.
This wave of emotions has made you wise.
You substitute the urge,
Watching and breathing, and extinguishing
That burning flame that left you in debt
To the enigma of sorrow still flourishing.
And the battle is now being won,
'Cause it was dementia that captured your sun.

My First Song

As I sit at my doorstep,
As I watch the people come and go,
I clutch my broom –
'Cause it's the only possession I have.
As old and frail as I am,
There's really nothing that matters now,
For I see, I see,
I see a hope in the future,
Though everything seems so dark.
I see a future that has something to hold,
I see a hope that will remain
Joyful for ever and ever.
I know they know not the end.
My home
Is nothing but an old garage
That's all torn apart.
Even though everything seems so dark,
I see a future that has something to hold,
I see hope that will remain
Joyful for ever and ever.
I know they know not the end!

Tenacious Taciturnity

My love,
My sweet love,
The starlight reminds me of a romantic evening
I wish to share with you.
Roses remind me of what I am missing,
Not being next to you!

I want to speak to you all day and all night,
But the world gets in the way.
You're there and I'm here,
But still, in the silence of my room
I dream only of you.
I'll write to you every day
So long as you write back,
And I'll be here if you need me.

The dawn was soon,
Hiding behind the sun was the moon.
I watched the velvet sky turn
As I watched the earth burn.
Outside where the company screams,
Inside when the soul divides
Heart and mind teams,
And the spirit resides.

A whisper in the night,
I love you.
A gentle halo,
A need replenished,
Fear anguished,
And now,
'What now?'

Labour of Love

With each passing day,
Thoughts of you grow distant,
But my heart just won't let me say
The words that mean it's over,
'Cause for an instant
My world seemed so perfect.
I will never keep a secret
From you.

You and I are beyond that now,
And I'm hoping that somehow
You'll also be thinking of me
And let this love be.

It is said that
The best things in life are free.
They are.
You need not strive to create anything,
You need only claim them.
So come and claim
The love
That is already yours.

Time always seems to catch up on me
When I feel like I've all the time in the world.
Hours fly
And days go by.

The times when I'm having fun
With new friends,
I feel as if my life is a stage,
A bridge from here to the ever after.

Misconception weighs me down,
Keeps me searching for
The little things in life that matter to me
Like the symphony of the triumph of love.

It's not pain we are battling with,
But happiness.
To trust that in the end,
We've done the right thing.

My Saddest Dream

If you could only know what I'm going through,
Not being able to be with you.
Now, you say you hate school,
And I'm loving it –
8.30 lectures till 4.30 in the afternoon –
Not 'cause I have class all day,
But would rather be at college than do nothing all day.
Some say it's sad,
But then again,
There is nothing worse than an idle mind.
It's wearing me out, I know.
But again
My wondering heart holds on to the hope of a better
   tomorrow.

The life I'd imagined
Is the life I dare to dream,
And in dreaming I made a wish
And looked at my star.
The star carried my dream to heaven
And there stood God,
The High Almighty.
And I bowed my head
In dread
Of what he would say.
And if I may
I'd stand on a bay.
Gazing into the ocean depth,

And then I leapt
Into the misty waters
As if nothing else matters!

…That was my saddest dream.

Here's wishing you a lovely week.

Love,

Grace

Vital Impression

The birds fly in flocks outside my bedroom window.
It makes me smile to see the wondrous life outside
  myself.
I live on the top floor
And I love to gaze outside my window
At the birds and the sky.
It may be cloudy sometimes,
But there's a small fountain below,
And the sound of the water splashing on the pavement
Washes me clean and clear of all troubling thoughts
And it leads me back to myself,
Me,
The only person I'll ever need.

Warm thoughts of you are enough to keep me warm this winter!

Grace

Wishful Whispers

To me you're a *national symbol*,
A *great hero* for the youth.
'Cause whatever undertaking you pursue,
Your heart follows
And your life obeys,
Somewhat like a disciple
With a creed to progress.
And I know the stars above
Just watch over you,
Day and night,
As I would
If I was by your side!

   Love,

   Grace

Selfless Salvage

Gone are the days
When I used to hold a teddy in my sleep,
When the feelings of unseen love were my rays
To shine through my heart and keep
The only state I knew – loneliness.

Then fear took me by surprise,
Like the pangs of Hell's greyhound,
Howling at me when I rise,
Grabbing at my newly found
Confidence that surpassed reality.

Smiling at my fate,
I closed my eyes – arms open wide,
And made a date
That took me for a ride
Round and down into a black hole – despair.

Defending what I now call pride,
I called out into the night
To my love to be by my side,
But he seemed out of sight.
Then I put my heart on the firing line.

Guns pointed at me.
I yelled as loud as I could –
'Let me be…Let me be…'
But then they didn't hear me – even if they could,
It was my life or theirs.

It then dawned on me that life is a destination,
Like our being is to live and die,

Like a rose dressed so delicately
In its fragrant velveteen petals,
Will one day wither and die.
Nature is changeable, even though being isn't.
And the instant of destiny is the moment
Our being meets our nature.
It's up to us to determine our destiny.

Love,

Grace

Eagles' Eyes

So the guns fired
As my heart tired.
Eyes cast towards heaven's gate,
But it was too late!

The flames of hell
As I heard the bell:
'Ding…dong…ding…dong…'
It was all wrong!

I let out a sigh,
As my body gave way.
I must say,
The time was nigh!

I awoke to find you
Gazing at me.
Happiness slipped through
And I knew
You would be true!

Hope you had a good day and that you are fine.

Love,

Grace

The Eternal Embrace

I lay on my bed and put on some music…Jeff Buckley.
I turned on my side and closed my eyes,
Left arm listless, and stretched under my right arm,
Right arm under my pillow.
It felt like someone was holding me,
And I felt safe and secure in this embrace.

I took a breath and let myself go,
Swimming with the music
As time passed by.
The energy lost in the day,
Recaptured by this embrace,
Wiped away the last trace
Of stress –
This was the Eternal Embrace.

Thoughts
The thought process is of limited nature –
The you who thought it wouldn't
Is only a thought that thought it couldn't.

Limited old patterns,
Which ruled your life,
Show that there is a better and higher
Destiny within you that exists
In your true being.

Knowing who you are
Only means that you know who you are not,
And this is the key to the real you.

Appearances could be deceptive,
Just as actions can be misinterpreted.

The moment you realise your true worth
Is the moment your dreams will come true,
'Cause you can't fool yourself for ever.

Darling, have a nice evening and take care 'cause I care!

Love,

Grace

Phenomenal Promise

I'm glad you like the poems I write to you. Writing poetry has become a part of me. Each day, with a little inspiration, I put the pen to the paper. You are my sole/soul inspiration. Thank you.

> Whenever you feel low –
> And being alive can sometimes hurt –
> I'll be the one to show
> What treasures you own inside.
>
> I'll take your place,
> And speed away from it all.
> Your face left a trace
> Of shyness –
>
> But I liked it,
> Because I now am sure
> Of the reasons I have to want to be with you –
> I'm sure of you!
>
> It's a very scary feeling,
> But I can't stop believing.
>
> Lies beneath these hopes
> Is the thought of you;
> Your strength in those deep-set eyes,
> For promises
> To finally one day set me free!

Hope Asunder

Help me out of this mire,
Whisper words of desire.
Love lost and love found;
People all around,
Each to their own,
In this town.

Right now, I'm blindly pessimistic
About the commitment.
It's hard to be optimistic,
About the elusive, everlasting love meant
Between you and I.

Mansions of dreams built in the air,
Gold-plated rims abound;
All territories tear,
With scores of frenzied hearts to be found;
All hearts beating silent drumbeats to the grave.

A rainbow stands for a promise,
The beginning then sees
Its demise.
And in looking at the rainbow,
Flowers and bees,
The cold wind will blow…
Blow your heart to mine!

Love,

Grace

Fortunate Affection

Today I was staring out my bedroom window –
It as drizzling a little, and onto the rooftop
Came flying a crow.

I watched its every move.
It looked at me
And I whispered to it,
'I love you…'

It then perched on the roof's edge.
Moments passed by,
And it said in its own secret tongue,
'I love you…'
Three sounds that meant it, I know.

It then flew away
And disappeared into the corner.
You know,
Birds have the secret tongue of angels,
And this was my revelation
Of the crow that spoke.

My Darling

I hang my head over the railing,
My spirit is now reaching out
To you without a doubt.

It's been so lonely,
Bearing my heart to you openly.
I come alive,
Each time I just survive,
When you say my name,
'Cause you're not here with me.

Seeing is believing.
My heart is reliving.
My mind is receiving
Mixed thoughts about you.

Left out in the cold,
Without the soul that I sold,
No more room to be bold,
No meaning left to behold.

Feeling like a swamp,
Drowning in earth's tears.
You are my lamp,
All that I need to get me through the years.

…sending you all my love,

Grace

Empty Words, Empty Promises

My fondest memories are found in your eyes:

Guess I won't hear wedding bells now.
Trying to understand what you've done,
Believing that the vow
Was nothing but a spark that's now gone.

It's for the best.
It was a vivid apprehension.
Guess I didn't pass the test.
So my heart folds in conclusion.

The days seem longer.
Tell me what I've done.
The nights I flounder
'Cause thoughts are on the run.

I'm not looking
For a hurried love.
I'm not booking
My place up above.

I'm just realising –
Empty words, empty promises.
How it hurts to be fantasising,
'Cause my heart just reminisces.

    Grace

Eternal Embrace

From this moment no dream will do without you.

1) My dearest thoughts resides and is found in your eyes.

2) My most exciting dream began and ended with you.

3) My most true desire became a fire with you.

4) My happiest moment is easy to remember with you.

5) My closest comfort turned into a reality with you.

6) My inner strength came from believing, and reliving my days with you.

7) My most passionate emotion was born with you.

8) My most sincere glimpse of love came from you.

9) My most promising imagination were directed and inspired with you.

10) My most certain sense of belonging was felt with you.

11) My most apparent self-esteem was cultivated by you.

12) My most vivid experience was given life with you.

13) My most genuine encounter was decided with you.

14) My most enticing temptation was caused by you.

15) My disheartening search for someone ended with you.

16) My one and only wish came true with you.

17) My strangest tears flowed and were betrothed with you.

18) My quest for wholeness came from, and was seen by you.

19) My deepest intuition turned into a song with you.

20) My sweetest smile came into being with you.

21) My most relaxed ideas existed throughout with you.

22) My most wonderful adventure was disguised with you.

My Life…

A sea of tears
Washed through my days.
A few, but again,
So many years,
Clouded by an angel,
Who hid the sun's rays.

Life is too short.
So you say we've got
No time to waste.
But listen to my thought –
I'd like to give life a taste.

Laughter escapes
As time reflects,
Happy memories engulfs
This tide of loneliness like a vault –

Tell me if ever love's power
Can be enough to remedy,
To erase the pain like a blossom flower.
Life like sweet telepathy.

The Bridge

As I journey through my emotions,
Full of serious notions –
Some made me laugh,
Some made me cry,
And sometimes –

I'm drowning in the depths
Of wondering why;
The tears of a forbidden existence
That ends with you
And begins with you,
'Cause for ever will be

The bridge that became of me.

There's No Price I Won't Pay

For you are my comfort and strength.
You built me up from my wasted ruin

And made me who I am.
I am who I am now because of you.
Times between us were rough to begin with.
The price I had to pay for it

Made me lose my mind.
But still,
I love you.
And if I have to lose
My mind again for you,
I'll do all I can
'Cause you are

My everlasting love.
To the heights of the unknown,
Even to the bottomless pit of reason
'Cause I love you so much –
Until for ever will be
The spark in my heart for you,
And the fire you see in my eyes.

So Sad

I keep watching reruns
In my life:
Many a strife,
Many a sorrow,
Sometimes there is no tomorrow.

So I take a walk down memory lane,
Down to the sea shore,
And there fall on my knees,
And reach to the heavens – therein to implore.

As I gaze at the endlessness
Of the waters,
Washing away all past thoughts that are reminiscence
Like a transition of mishaps that falters,

Longing and groping –
Reaching out to fill this emptiness within,
While all my dreams still hoping,
Until sunset sets in –

All by myself –
And dazed by the piercing sound of birds singing
A hand touches and embraces me like my other half,
And I'm comforted again as shivers up my spine tingling.

Two Extremes

When joy and reality clash,
Hearts divide and loneliness conquers
Past emotions,
Past ideals —
New life.

From Now Until For Ever

I could stand by your side,
With all my love to reside
In your heart to keep,
From now
Until for ever.

One...

Together you and me
Amidst the clouds,
Together, as one,
We will fall
Down to earth
And embrace the
Love we've found.

Where Were You?

Thought I saw
A lifetime in your eyes.
Thought you really knew,
Thought you really cared.
Where were you?

Blue

Reminds me of the clear sky,
Looks like the colour of your eyes –
Blue,
'Cause you're true.

When there's nothing left –
Please, please, hurry home –
Now I know just what lonely really means
My dear Lapis – S – ring
Stolen away –
That moment of frustration –
And I've been torn –
Wondering if you can still feel my heart?
Blue stone – O most precious jewel –
My beauty –
What will become of luck
Now that you are gone?
There won't be a loving kiss goodnight anymore,
There won't be another like you –
But here in my heart,
Memories are for all time!

Vindication

Lately I've been disconcerted.
The pain of rejection
Left me disenchanted
And blew away life's fruition.

I yelled that I shall not concede
To become depressive,
Or even worse to precede,
To what I have become – apprehensive.

Solitude

Gazing into the water,
The lights reflect
The turmoil in my head – slaughter.

My heart to perfect…

Overwhelmed by memories,
No energy left in me,
In despair over recurring reveries,
Longing for these eyes of mine to see.

Solace…

There was a time,
Words hurt more than reality's mystery,
With nothing but a rhyme
From a philosopher's history –

The catch-22 is now obvious –
Empty words and lies.
His reasons were suspicious,
And it's tragic how my heart just dies.

Adversity

Feelings come and feelings go,
It's sad but true.
If you'd only have let me show
The thoughts I have just for you.

It now seems lost,
Days just pass by,
And I still count the cost
I've had to pay for being shy.

Now you just look on,
Not even a glance.
I feel torn,
'Cause you wouldn't even give me a chance.

You're not to blame,
Guess I'm not your type.
So this dying flame –
I'll just smoke away on my pipe.

Release

Seeing is believing,
Reality is just reliving,

Mind is a mess,
Heart is trying to erase,

What could have been between you and me.

Tragedy

I am longing
For that gentle caress,
That unification of knowing,
The wonderful experiencing of a love
That life will never erase.

Memories

I know nothing I could say
Could heal
Your broken heart.

I feel lost when
I think about you,
And my mind is in conflict about
My need to love you…

I do love you.

Please believe me, my friend.
I know I can
Ease the pain with my words,
But I could never remain
The same,

Because…

You're everything I've believed in.

Now

Presently, I've been sitting,
My mind
In a merry-go-round.

Lately I've been walking
And I've realised
I could not have managed it
Any other way.
My circumstances have changed,
Because now I am myself,
Someone like you, somehow.
Now I'm writing
And saying to myself …?

You...

A role model,
An elegant touch of
That humanity inside you.

Your compassion and the loving caress
Of your glance,
Added to this new day,
Your assurance,
Making it bliss,
And everything had meaning:

You.

I'm still adjusting
To the fact that you're
No longer here.

And as my hope for this world
Is uncertain,
Your presence remains felt;
That is all you were:

You.

Me...

I amaze myself at how
You've changed my life.
Seeing you as an inspiration,

Makes me true
To myself and others.
Believing in everything
You did
Makes me a stronger person –

The person I longed to be,
That is, me.
And all that I will be
Depended on you,

My guide and solace,
You are now beyond –
Somewhere far away –
But you will live for ever
Inside me.

True

The basic concepts governing –
Like understanding, love and hope –
All embraced by you,

All embraced by you.
And you became the epitome
Of the great and true;

A blessing to the world,
To the downhearted,
The suffering, and most of all,
To the true.

All that's left to bear
Is the cross you bore all along,
Whilst imparting
All that is
True to us.

Since

All that mattered,
All that matters,
Since

This is what you left behind:
Lessons for the wise
And the laymen alike,

For the bold and the meek,
The jolly and the sad.
The path you walked

Descended from
The spiritual giants,
For your deeds proclaimed

Louder than words,
All that is certain,
Solid and precious

In the hearts of all men,
Even though we are
Not fully aware of this,

Since…

How?

For being you,
For the love,
For the understanding,
For the hope you instilled,
For a better tomorrow,
For a happier world,
For a prosperous future.

It's difficult to find someone,
Someone else like you.
I sometimes feel that
I don't want someone else
To take your place –
I loved you 'cause you loved me.

But sometimes God,
Not man,
Has control.
God took you away from
The world we both knew.

How can I hold on
To the hope without you?

Oblivion

I never anticipated
A day that spelt
'Never again'.

Never again shall I see
Your lovely face to reassure me.
Never again will we share the same breath
That sustains life in this universe.

Perhaps in the afterlife,
We shall never again say goodbye.
It's inevitable that one sad day,
We shall all have to say farewell,
But we don't know when,
Nor how,
And this to me is
Oblivion.

Days

The pangs of thirst of wild animals,
Making every step a torment,
Was the fearful jungle I lived in.

The pain you endured
Was nothing compared
To anything I've experienced.

Your strength made me realise
That there is a new,
Different and better way
To face the day.

You gave meaning to my days,
And they became life-enriching
Because of you.
And the lessons to be learnt
With the will
You rooted in me.

Thoughts

Thought I saw a lifetime
In your eyes.
Thought I knew
Your destiny.
Thought we could pull through
Together.
'Cause you were always
In my prayers.
Thoughts like these
Keep me still,
In a state of shock and disbelief.
I believe in you and I pledge
My love for you.

Thoughts I know can't tell me
When or if I learn to live
Without you.
At least I know
I feel such a great loss.

Conflict

I hate you for knowing him,
I hate you for being with him,
But the real reason I hate you
Is for not introducing him to me.
He was my kind of perfect guy,
The epitome of my dream,
The light at the end of the tunnel.
I remember the first time I set eyes on him,
He was with you,
But I didn't care,
It really didn't matter,
But now reality sets in,
Sinks into my thick skull:
He was with you all along.
I guess I don't stand a chance any more.
It would now never be enough
For me to have him
All to myself,
'Cause he is with you.
I tried to be hopeful,
I tried to smile –
Now my smile just seems out of place.
I know it's over –
What might have been
Could never be.
I clutch at my broken heart,
A heart that once sang,
Sang when I saw him.
There's no more might,
In this one dead body.
I pray now that my mind,
My secret hiding place,

My solace,
The true inner strength
I depend on,
Will give me a reason to love again.
But oh!
How I desired you,
How I dreamt of you,
How I worshipped the ground
On which you walked.
How you carried yourself,
Your face –
Oh! –
That lovely face of yours,
For life to bestow on me
Such a blessing –
You.
Oh! It's such a tragedy!
Slowly but surely
I know
That my tears will cease
When there is no more sorrow.
No doubt that I cared deeply for you,
But you just didn't,
Couldn't or wouldn't
Care for me
Like I did for you.
The present is a catastrophe,
The future is bleak,
My soul is tired
Of the longing
I wished to bring into this reality.
Maybe,
Just maybe, we could be friends,
But again –
What use and what's the point
Of that kind of consolation?
It's been my way
Not to foresee disaster,

And this time
I played myself,
A loser in the conquest,
A timid soul who needs someone,
But that someone had to be him.
But 'cause it will never be,
I'm drowning in misery.
This is the price I have to pay
For my carefree attitude.
I now see the implications
Though try hard not to.
I feel defeated and sad
To see you.
Once it brought me such joy;
Now it only brings me pain.
I'll get over you, I know.
I'll make it through
To see another day,
A brand new day,
Filled with promise and happiness,
But I still can't get over
What became of me and you,
Strangers in this world.
There is no need for sorrow,
No place for the memories,
'Cause all I know and see
Is your face, your beauty –
All this and more, here in my head,
This head full of thoughts of you.

Moments

It's a secret that will amaze you.
I'd like you to keep it
Just between you and me.
When life is a stage
And we are all actors
Playing our part,
Then something hidden in me
Says that the stage is empty
Without you in my life.

> You can either live for the moment or live in the moment. I live in the moment, but here in my head I just live *for* the moment.

Happiness

It seems funny
When it's not sunny,
To feel peaceful;
And when my mind
Is like
Crippled words –
Blind but still seeing,
Deaf but still listening,
Asleep but alert,
Grasping at every moment,
Every second
Of the surest miracle.
Of happiness.

May 4th

I know there's a presence
With me all the time.
Some call it 'angel',
Some say 'Him',
Whom I know I couldn't do without.

Yesterday I cried when I heard,
'So how long is it going to take you
To get over me?'
I stared still into the night,
My eyes shut in disbelief.
My heart was shattered,
My mind screamed,
'I could never get over you!'
The tears of my lonely heart
Spilt over the pillow.

Was He also going to break my heart?

Fists clenched over my chest
As if to save my broken heart
From falling to pieces,
Legs folded over my arms,
Like a baby in its mother's womb.

What was once a time zone
Of love and happiness
Turned into sorrow,
A sorrow so deep that it cut
Right through my very soul,
The essence of my being.